WANDA-ANNE MARS

NEVER BROKEN

**The Ultimate Guide to Staying Positive At All Times,
Discover the Ways on How to Have Relentless Optimism
As a Key to Overflowing Happiness and Success in Life**

Descrierea CIP a Bibliotecii Naţionale a României
WANDA-ANNE MARS
   NEVER BROKEN. The Ultimate Guide to Staying Positive
At All Times, Discover the Ways on How to Have Relentless
Optimism As a Key to Overflowing Happiness and Success in
Life / Wanda-Anne Mars – Bucharest: Editura My Ebook, 2020
   ISBN

WANDA-ANNE MARS

NEVER BROKEN

The Ultimate Guide to Staying Positive At All Times, Discover the Ways on How to Have Relentless Optimism As a Key to Overflowing Happiness and Success in Life

My Ebook Publishing House
Bucharest, 2020

TABLE OF CONTENTS

INTRODUCTION

Optimism is assuming the best outcome is possible. Pessimism assumes the worst outcome is inevitable. These two different types of people view life entirely differently. However, there is little doubt that optimists are happier, healthier, and generally more successful in all aspects of their lives. A little optimism goes a long way.

Many people believe that one's past determines one's level of optimism or pessimism. To a certain extent, that is true. Children raised to think positively are far more likely to remain optimists than children raised with negativism. However, as adults, we always have choices. Whether we spend our time making lemonade out of lemons or complain about the shortage of lemons is always choice. While optimists see possibilities, pessimists see problems.

Pessimism is a mindset that we can change. This will happen when we want more out of life and when we believe we can achieve it. While negative thoughts keep us focused on roadblocks and reasons not to act, optimism and positive thinking open our mind to new opportunities. It fills us with the belief that life can provide us with more. Optimists don't expect guarantees, but they are willing to risk roadblocks and failure for the *chance* at success. They see every reason why they should try for happiness.

It is this belief and mindset that determines the quality of their lives, not their ability, luck, or fate.

Optimists never see themselves as victims of circumstances. They understand things can go wrong at any time, but they also know how many good opportunities are possible. So, they learn to deal with obstacles to reach their goals and dreams. For optimists, obstacles are lessons to be learned on the road to success.

Optimists feel in control of their lives, while pessimist are certain that life controls them.

Everyone can become more optimistic, happier, and more successful. All you have to do is expect more out of life and realize that more is possible. Expectations have a way of being self- fulfilling. Those who view the glass as half-full have an excellent chance of enjoying a life of abundance because that is their expectation of life. Pessimists who see the glass as half-empty may spend a lifetime suffering from thirst.

This book attempts to explain the mindset and benefits of optimism, and how to increase positive thinking for a better life. Regardless of your circumstances, you can make positive changes that lead to greater success. The way you think determines how you act. And your actions determine whether you are guided by optimism or negativism.

CHAPTER 1

WHAT IS OPTIMISM?

We all have a vague idea that optimism is good – seeing the glass as half full and making lemonade from lemons. Optimists see success as their right. It's there if they are willing to work for it. Many people, however, believe it's some innate ability we are born with. Either you have it, or you don't.

Nothing could be further from the truth. While optimism can be partially genetic (if you were raised in an optimistic family, the odds are you will have that trait), it can also be learned.

Optimism is a mindset that believes in the possibility of a good outcome. Equally as important, it understands that there are hurdles along the way. Life is filled with the unexpected. No one gets *everything* he or she wants, and optimists don't expect it. However, they build the type of resilience that encourages them to keep trying. Optimists are not guided by failure. There may be many rainy days, but eventually, the sun will always come out. If that glass of water gets spilled, it can always get refilled. That's how an optimist approaches life. He or she may stumble but will always get back up.

Research has found that being optimistic will enhance your quality of living and your health when compared to pessimists. It encourages flexible thinking, creativity, and greater problem-solving capability. All of that decreases stress and ensures a healthier body.

Let's take a look at how optimists behave when compared to pessimist, because there is a significant difference.

1. Optimists know that they are responsible for their own life, with all of its ups and downs. They don't depend on others to feel good, successful, or attractive. They are the masters of their own fate.

To be clear, it is not necessary for an optimist to be overly successful or attractive. An optimist can be an unassuming person, living a simple life, and extremely content with everything he or she has. To him or her, that *is* success.

2. Optimists associate with other optimists. The people you associate with impact your life in many ways. It has been said that we are the sum of the five people whom we associate with the most. Optimists choose their friends wisely.

Pessimists will, unfortunately, drag you down with their negative thinking. It's almost inevitable. Some people can complain about anything – the world in general, the job, a meal at a restaurant, a movie … the list doesn't end. This attitude invariable rubs off on others and is best avoided if you are an optimist. And if success is your goal, know that the number one trait of successful people is positive thinking. A positive outlook is the sure way to get through hard times.

While you can't avoid everyone, it's best to surround yourself with as much optimism as possible. Look for people who share your mindset.

3. Optimism can uncover and reveal opportunities. Both optimists and pessimists see problems for the logical reason that life is filled with them. The difference is, a pessimist uses the problems as an excuse to do nothing, while the optimist sees them as an opportunity. Let's say John and Jane want to start their own business, while will take $10,000 capital. John thinks, "I don't have that kind of money. What's the use?" Jane thinks, "Okay, what should I do to get an extra $10,000?" Jane, the optimist, sees an opportunity for some creative problem-solving. She sees possibilities where John sees roadblocks. It's not difficult to guess which of the two will be more successful.

4. Optimist calls for self-confidence, something we will explore in greater detail in a different chapter. Optimists are confident enough not to be guided by the opinions of others. It's clear to them that they will never please everyone, so they don't bother trying. They rely on their own judgment. If they make mistakes, they take full ownership and responsibility of correcting them.

5. To take the foregoing point a step further, optimist don't indulge in blaming others when things go wrong. They leave the complaining to pessimists. Optimists are mainly concerned with understanding what happened and how to improve it next time.

To iterate an important point, optimism seeks solutions, not excuses.

6. Gratitude is an important component of optimism. This grateful attitude allows optimist to see the good things in life and hope for even better. A pessimist will complain about his or job while the optimist will be grateful to be working. It's the optimist's attitude that will make it easier for him or her to seek something better.

7. Optimism is never ruled by anger. Life can be very unfair, and pessimists will make a point to list each and every instance. Your family may be not as rich as your neighbor, others may be more successful, and your sibling may be more beautiful and drive a better car. There are a lot of things to be envious and angry about. But what does it solve? Anger fuels non-action and complacency like few other emotions. Optimists move beyond and attempt to create change instead of indulging in complaining and anger.

Optimism, as already stated, is fueled by what we do have, not what we lack. The optimist sees clean water, safe housing, a beautiful garden, food, and innovation as something to be grateful for. We have more than any other generation in history, yet pessimists still find reasons to complain. Some hold on to their anger as if it were a lifeline. Optimists understand that anger acts like a chain, making it impossible to move forward. Positive thinking is a choice; so is holding on to negativity.

8.   You may think that optimists expect life to be easy. It would make sense, but the exact opposite is true. An optimist *knows* how difficult and unfair life can be. As a result, he or she is mentally prepared. They develop the resilience that lets them cope with adversity instead of wallowing in it. They *know* they won't get every job, every romantic partner, every wish fulfilled, so adversity doesn't stop them from moving ahead and trying again. An optimist plays the odds; he or she knows eventually, success will happen.

It is that willingness never to give up that separates the optimist from the rest. It's the very essence of optimism.

Psychologists agree that it is virtually impossible to be successful without optimism. One of the reasons is that optimist will work harder (for years, if necessary) to achieve their dream.

Only someone who is certain of a positive outcome would be willing to put in such an effort. Regardless of how many roadblocks he or she encounters, he or she never loses sight of what may be possible at the end of the road. Optimists see the rainbow at the end, not the rain along the way.

It's impossible to be optimistic without positive thinking, but there is a small, yet important, difference. The positive thinker says, "I think I can." The optimist says, "I will." They are both driven, but the optimist's engine is slightly more enhanced.

That is the reason the optimist is willing to put in years of effort without giving up. He or she is usually guided by a deep hunger, or passion, for success, whether personal or professional. They know exactly what they want out of life. Not striving toward a goal is simply not an option for the optimist.

In a delightful movie, "Mrs. 'Arris Goes to Paris," Mrs. Harris is a middle-aged domestic working for a very wealthy lady. The lady owns several magnificent Dior dresses, which Mrs. Harris greatly admires. But she doesn't stop at mere admiration. Mrs. Harris becomes determined to own her Dior creation before she dies. She spends years saving pennies from her servant's wages. All of her friends tell her she is crazy. What does a maid want with a Dior dress? But, Mrs. Harris has her dream. When she finally saves up enough money, she travels to Paris, where she encounters a few adventures. And she finally gets to visit Dior and order her dress.

With her life's dream in tow, she travels back to London and her job as a maid. Will she ever get to wear her dream dress? No one knows. That's not the point. Mrs. Harris wanted to *own* a Dior, and she finally realized her dream, after years of hard work. Mrs. Harris is proof you can't keep an optimist down.

CHAPTER 2

BENEFITS OF OPTIMISM

Before we discuss how optimism can and will lead to greater success in all areas of your life, it's important to consider the actual physical health benefits that positive thinking can bring about. Many studies have shown how optimism can help individuals cope with illness and maintain better overall health. Your mind and body work as a unit. When your mind is well-tuned, your body reaps the benefits.

Optimism and Heart Health

The term "broken heart" has some literal truth. Stress, anxiety, and depression can indeed bring on heart problems. The lack of those symptoms, on the other hand, can bring about greater heart health. Optimism is heart-healthy.

In a particular study, 309 patients were evaluated prior to coronary artery bypass surgery. This included an evaluation of their mental state as related to pessimism, optimism, and self-esteem. Six months following the surgery, it was found that pessimists were twice as likely to require further hospital treatment than the optimistic group.

Another study of angioplasty patients revealed that pessimists were three times as likely to suffer a heart attack than optimists.

Blood Pressure

Numerous studies have confirmed that optimism impacts blood pressure in a very positive way. A study in Finland involved over 600 middle-aged men who had normal blood pressure at the onset of the study. After observing this group for three years, researchers determined the optimists were three times less likely to suffer from high blood pressure than pessimists. The likely reason is that optimists spend less time worrying and more time taking positive action.

These studies have been repeated many times with the same results. People who lean toward positive thinking rather than negative are far more likely to be calmer and less likely to suffer from high blood pressure.

Infections

Anyone can suffer from an infection. Infections are generally caused by invading foreign organisms that infect the body and continue to multiply. Sometimes, the body will handle these invaders itself. Other times, it may succumb to disease through a weakened immune system.

In a 2006 study, 193 healthy men and women were given a respiratory virus. The results were that those volunteers judged to have a positive outlook were less like to develop signs of infections. Optimism can strengthen the immune system and help ward off diseases. Many people don't realize the full power of the mind.

Overall Health

In a two-year study relating to optimism and overall health, researchers evaluated 2,300 adults. At the end of the study, they determined that those adults with the most positive outlook had a greater likelihood of enjoying better overall health than their negative counterparts.

Optimism and Longevity

If optimism can improve people's health, the logical assumption would be that it can boost longevity, as well. This supposition was proven in two separate studies.

A 1960's study evaluated 839 people for optimism and overall health. These people were rechecked after 30 years. The results showed that optimists who'd increased their pessimism also increased their mortality rate. Those who remained optimistic or increased their level of optimistic had a lower mortality rate.

The second study during the same period involved 6,959 students who were evaluated for a 40-year period. At the end of the study, pessimists had a 42 percent higher death rate than the more positive thinking group.

A number of similar studies have confirmed the findings that an optimistic attitude can lead to better health and a longer life.

Optimism and Stress

Stress is one of the leading causes of death. A recent study showed that everyone, optimists and pessimists, experience stress. It's a part of life and can't be avoided. It's how an individual handles stress that is important. The same study revealed that optimists recovered much quicker from stress-related incidents than pessimists.

As a whole, optimists feel less stressed because they don't expect everything to go their way. They are mentally prepared to expect the best, but when it doesn't happen, they keep trying. Their world doesn't fall apart because they are able to cope better. Adversity is seen as temporary in nature instead of a normal fact of life. Since optimists tend to be more hopeful and self-confident, they are also likely to try harder, take more risk, and thereby create more positive events in their lives than pessimists.

Optimists Are Better Leaders

The benefits of optimism go far beyond health. It is well-known that optimism is an essential characteristic of an effective leader, and there are logical reasons for this.

Optimists recognized opportunities and refuse to be victims of circumstances. During bad economic times, which can overwhelm pessimists, optimists find ways to start a business and provide jobs for other people. This would be impossible if a person were filled with worries about uncertainties.

Optimistic leaders communicate positivity to those around them and inspire trust and loyalty. People want to be around optimists. They not only encourage themselves to do more, they encourage those around them.

Pessimists can worry about every minute that could wrong, preventing them from even getting started. Optimists are confident in their ability to handle the details and focus on the larger picture of solving problems. They refuse to be stopped by a "This is impossible" mentality.

Optimists are willing to work to achieve their goals. Because they know they will face obstacles, these roadblocks are not deterrents, but challenges. People are willing to follow optimists because they understand that the optimist will work to improve a situation. Optimists aren't just confident, they inspire confidence in others. That is why they make effective managers.

Optimism Encourages Persistence

Because optimists don't expect guarantees, they do not give up easily when life becomes bleak. They know success *is* possible, so giving up is rarely an option for them. Success is simply a matter of how and when instead of if. Most entrepreneurs have failed several times before reaching their goal, but they don't let that stop them. And once they reach their original goal, they continue to reach further. For an optimist, there are no limits. Only possibilities.

Optimism and Anxiety

Many studies have shown how optimism serves as a "balm" against anxiety. One of the most prevalent causes of anxiety is irrational thinking: if you are a pessimist, you see two people quietly talking, you assume they are making fun of you; the boss just passed your desk and didn't even acknowledge you, so you assume she hates you.

People suffering from anxiety hold these thoughts even when there is not an iota of evidence to support them. Their mindset is to fear and expect the worst. Anxiety is pessimism in its extreme form. Obviously, the best way to combat anxiety is to strive for optimism.

If you are used to expecting the worst, it can be difficult to change that mindset quickly. You can, however, achieve greater optimism by taking small steps. Ask yourself if there is any basis for your thoughts. Give others the benefit of doubt.

While it may not sound pleasant, but ask yourself if you are really important enough for people to be talking behind your back. Most people are too wrapped up in themselves to give others that much thought. Ask yourself if there might be a reason for someone else's behavior that doesn't involve you at all. While optimism is out outward directed, pessimism is very inward-looking.

When you get into the habit of challenging irrational and pessimistic beliefs, they lose their grip. That's when you can slowly allow yourself to think more positively and lessen any feelings of anxiety.

CHAPTER 3

BOOST YOUR OPTIMISM
WHEN THE GLASS IS HALF-EMPTY

Life can be unpredictable and cruel. That's simply a fact. Optimists don't move through the day merely smelling the roses. Sometimes adversity can be real and overwhelming, even for positive thinkers. It's when the water in that glass begins to trickle south that we need our optimistic resources the most.

As a healthy body needs the occasional tune-up, so does the optimistic mind. Luckily, there are actions we can take to give our brain a needed boost when the world begins to look dark. Like a weak muscle, optimism can be strengthened and toughened.

Practice Gratitude

Gratitude is so important, it deserves its own chapter. This is a reminder when life seems to be lacking, it a good time to remind yourself of the things you *do* have. Never lose sight of the good things that surround you.

Imagine Yourself at Your Best

Expecting the best development in a situation is a natural inclination for optimists. But sometimes, it can be a strain. When that happens, resort to the old adage, "Fake it till you make it."

Find a quiet place and visualize the thing you want to happen becoming real.

See yourself on a job interview and getting an offer.

Perhaps you've been looking for a romantic partner with no success. You've been patient, knowing that not every approach will end in success. You've kept your thoughts positive. But at the moment, your energy is sapped. The only thing you can think of is spending every New Year's Eve alone for the rest of your life. Now, imagine a different scenario in your mind.

Close your eyes and visualize yourself brimming with confidence. You're looking fantastic and charismatic, George Clooney is eyeing you for guidance. Imagine as many details as possible as you approach someone, and she is smiling and interested. It turns out you two have a lot in common. When you ask her out, she eagerly accepts.

Creating your own reality in your mind will transfer to real life. It will keep you going until your imagination becomes real. Because as an optimist, you know it will eventually happen. Sometimes, you just need a little reminder.

Learn to Believe in Yourself Again

Your self-confidence is at a low point. This can happen to anyone. Don't pretend it's business as usual. Instead, admit that you are feeling low and then take steps to climb out of the doldrums.

1. We all have a comfort zone. When your confidence needs a push, move beyond that zone. Try something new, approach new people, put yourself in new and unfamiliar situations.

2. Be aware of any negative self-talk. Sometimes, your inner critic can come at you like a hungry pit bull. Your first step is to understand that this is not the real you. You need to separate yourself from this critic. Talk back to it. Tell your inner critic that he or she is wrong. He or she is lying, and you intend to treat yourself better. This may sound strange, but negative self-talk can be very powerful and keep us from moving forward. You need to create an opposing voice that is positive and on your side. Instead of accepting this pit bull, talk to yourself as you would to your best friend. Frankly, no one likes a critic.

3. When it feels you aren't getting anywhere, make a list of what you have accomplished and the times you have overcome obstacles. It's easy to lose sight of the positive when

we are in the grips of a lot of negative. This is a good time to remind yourself why you should be feeling proud of yourself.

4. Accept what you are going through. Life is a series of highs and lows. It's how you handle the low times that matters. Don't judge or blame yourself for having a rough time. Things will get better but accept the present for what it is.

Treat Yourself to a Reward

As you struggle to regain your optimism, reward any successes. Create more sweet moments in your life. Nice, little rewards just give you another reason to remain optimistic.

Get Physical

You know exercise can improve your body. It can do the same with your mind, as well. If pessimism is getting the better of you, walk, run, or join a gym. Just get moving.

Take Advantage of Nature's Bounties

We are meant to spend time outdoors. Walking along a beach, by a lake, or through a park is extremely uplifting. Enjoy nature with all of your sense. Inhale the scent of fresh grass, notice the colors and texture of the flowers. Hear the twitter of birds and the lapping of waves against the shore.

Don't Dwell on the Past or the Future

When we are vulnerable to pessimistic thinking, our mind can journey on a time machine to the past and the future. We can find ourselves dwelling on past mistakes or injustices or fret about what will happen next week or next year. We are living everywhere but in the present.

Remind yourself that you cannot change the past, and you don't know the future. Relish living in the present, instead, and enjoy all that you have. Everything else is meaningless. As someone once said, the past is gone and the future hasn't happened.

Commit to a Positive Habit

Good daily habits invariably lift our spirits. They help us feel in greater control of our lives and remind us what we are capable of. Whether it's a daily walk, yoga, or meditation, it's a win as long as you do something positive every day.

Get Involved

There are few things that makes people feel more positive than helping others and making a difference. Find a cause that interests you and become the catalyst for real change. It's a very powerful feeling.

CHAPTER 4

OPTIMISM AND RELATIONSHIPS

Relationships require work. No relationship will survive, especially for the long-term, if you won't put considerable effort into it. No one is perfect, and an optimist doesn't expect it. For him or her, what is important is that the positives outweigh the negatives.

That is the reason it is so difficult for a pessimist to maintain any type of relationship. A pessimist will focus on a single flaw or problem and decide that this will never work. He or she won't even put in the effort. Expecting perfection is the pessimist's ultimate downfall. Many pessimists spend a lifetime looking for the ideal mate as they end up alone and lonely.

When a couple has problems and is willing to discuss them or seek counseling, that is an optimistic approach. You see the possibility of better days ahead. Optimism is a way of thinking, and our relationships depend on our mindset.

Pessimists frequently view a successful relationship as all or nothing. It's either great or it's a failure. Unfortunately for them, their relationship all too often end in failures.

A great relationship doesn't just happen. Two people will be successful if they approach the relationship with optimism. That means understanding that every day won't be paradise. But every day *will* provide an opportunity for growth, warmth, and joy when approached positively. Let's be realistic. Not every relationship will make it. However, optimism provides you with opportunities to strengthen what you have and increase the changes that you will succeed. No guarantees, mind you, but the chances greatly increase. It's the pessimist that looks for guarantees before trying. The optimist knows better.

When it comes to relationships, attitude is the primary ingredient. Just for a moment, imagine yourself around your good friends. Do you nag them about the way they dress? Do you fret every time your friend doesn't compliment you? Do you do things with your friends because *they* enjoy it and you enjoy their company?

This might be a good time to remember that your partner is also your friend. You're always delighted and supportive of your friends, right? If you continuously feel put upon or resentful when you are with your partner, perhaps your attitude could use a tune-up.

You can take your relationship to a much closer level with a positive attitude. Your partner will feel nurtured and appreciated. He or she will look forward to spending more time with you.

We have already pointed out that expecting perfection spells certain doom for a relationship. Instead, look for the good qualities in your partner and try to shrug off some of the others. Negotiate the rest.

Every relationship has those "other" qualities. Someone who leaves clothes lying around, spends too much money, or forgets anniversaries. Annoying? Absolutely. But your relationship can erode quickly if you make those things the focus. Instead, turn your mind to the positives and remember your partner's good qualities.

This should be a conscious effort to shirt your way of thinking. And then verbalize your thoughts to your partner. Tell him or her how much you love his or her cooking, sense of humor, or willingness to put up with your family. Appreciate it when he or she brings you some coffee or a beer. Often times we forget to be grateful for the little things.

It can be difficult to focus on the daily positives when you're worried about losing your job, the mortgage is late, and your teen just brought home a note from the principal. It will be easier if you share your thoughts with your partner and discuss positive solutions to your problem.

Like most couples, you probably celebrate life's major milestones, such as anniversaries and birthdays. Why not bring some positivity into your day and celebrate the small things, as well? Enjoy a dinner out just because it's Wednesday. Tuck a surprise note into your partner's pocket after a night of excellent romance. It's easy to notice problems and ignore the good things.

Think of your relationship as a bank account. The more optimism you deposit, the larger and better it will grow. If all you do is make withdrawals, you will find yourself broke sooner or later.

Instead of hoping for the best, some couples seem to expect the worst. Your spouse comes home late, he must be having an affair. Because your partner didn't return a phone call immediately, he or she surely hates you. Optimism always considers the possibility of a good explanation. Interestingly, when we expect good things to happen in our relationship, we usually get it. Conversely, when we expect negative things, that's also what we end up with. Our attitude has a habit of becoming self-fulfilling.

Try reframing a negative thought in your mind. "He's late again. He's been working hard, so I'll make sure he has a nice dinner." This is not to suggest you wear rose-colored glasses and ignore reality. But it's best not to create a negative reality without facts. And without facts, why assume the worst?

The more optimistic our thoughts are, the more positively we will act. And those actions are the equivalent of making deposits into the optimism account. They always earn dividends.

How to Infuse Your Relationship with More Optimism

Any optimist knows that success requires work. Even if your relationship is good, there are ways to kick it up a notch.

1.   Sure, our friends always listen when we complain about our partner. That's what friends are for. While venting is perfectly fine, try "venting" about some of the good things your partner has done. "Joe did the dishes without being asked." "Mary always has coffee ready when I get up." Think of your partner in positive terms rather than negative.

2.   Thank your partner for the small things. It's easy to take someone for granted.

3.   Share happy memories of the two of you. You had a great vacation, so why not keep the memories and positive feelings flowing. Take out the pictures and review the photographs. Share how much you enjoyed the different types of food and suggest you try a few different restaurants. Keep the good feelings alive.

4.   Many couples are busy discussing the daily grind of marriage – bills, work, repairs, kids, etc. - they forget to talk about themselves. Ask your partner questions such as, "When did you know you wanted to get married?" Or share your own memories. "I still remember my heart pounding when you first walked into that restaurant." These conversations are a great deal more optimistic than, "Why can't you ever pick up your socks?"

CHAPTER 5

WHY SOME PEOPLE ARE PESSIMISTS AND HOW TO STOP

To become more optimistic, it helps to understand why a pessimist clings to his or her beliefs. Only when you recognize certain traits will you be able to change them.

On the surface, it would seem optimists lead much better lives. If that is true, and it is, why do some people embrace pessimism?

If optimism is a mindset, pessimism can become one, as well. Pessimists view the world suspiciously as dangerous. Danger could be lurking around any corner. Not surprisingly, this very negative view of life can easily lead to depression and anxiety.

Pessimism doesn't just happen. Usually, it is meant to serve as protection against loss and disappointment. If a person experiences tremendous loss, especially when young, it can leave a tremendous imprint on the mind. The brain readily erects a protective shield against further pain. When viewed this way, pessimism can be very logical. Like a prey in a dangerous environment, pessimists are always on alert for danger.

Unfortunately, that danger can become real. Just as optimists draw good things toward them with their mind, pessimists can actually court bad luck with negative thinking. That only confirms their original pessimistic view of life as they say, "Aha. I knew it!"

What Makes a Pessimist?

1. Pessimists spend much of their life waiting for something better (as opposed to the optimist, who actively goes after what he or she wants.). The future is the pessimist's salvation. "I'll look for romance when I've lost ten pounds." "I'll start my own business after the kids have graduated." "I'll make more friends after I get a raise."

The reason given doesn't matter. Any excuse not to act will do. The pessimist is not one to take risks or face possible failure. Since life doesn't offer any guarantees, the pessimist spends much of his or her life hoping and wishing …

2. Instead of believing in themselves, pessimists rely on "things." They'll be fine if they get that house, that car, that suit. Chasing possessions is a lot easier than chasing dreams.

3. Pessimists avoid socializing with others. Loneliness, of course, only makes them feel more negative. But people involve risks, the possibility of rejection … all those things that the pessimist avoids.

4. Pessimists see themselves as victims of circumstances. It's their default position. Since life can be filled with so many obstacles, the pessimist feels out of control. He can't help what is

going on. Deep down, the pessimist feels helpless to change the things he would like to change. So, he does nothing.

5. Pessimists complain about the glass being half empty instead of making any attempt to fill it. This simply reinforces thenegative belief that the glass will always be unfilled.

6. Pessimists can blow small events way out of proportion in their own minds. What an optimist sees as a temporary setback is an invariable life-shaking event to the pessimist. A fender bender is proof that all people are careless and stupid. A suggestion from the boss to change a report means that the boss hates you and believes you to be totally incompetent. Pessimists thrive in crisis mode.

7. A pessimist judges himself according to other people. If his neighbor has a better car, he considers himself a failure. The optimist holds himself to his own standards.

8. Pessimists can also be their own worst judge and jury. They question every action and can find themselves "guilty" if perfection isn't achieved. Optimists are not concerned about perfection; they will continue trying even if they know they may falter. It's the trying that is crucial, not the result. This is a critical point. If perfection is the only gauge of success, no one would continue to try.

Moving from Pessimism to Optimism

On the surface, optimists aren't any different from pessimists. They can look alike, have the same ability, and yes, the same dreams. So, what makes them different? Attitude. Optimists are motivated by possibilities and will act to make them a reality. Pessimists are guided by fear and will act to keep those fears from happening.

The good news is, attitude can be changed. It won't happen overnight. The first step is to realize that *you* control your thoughts and actions. With each positive action you take, you move closer toward optimism.

1. Many optimists don't even realize that negativity has taken over their lives. It's become a natural, safe way of thinking. Consciously consider alternative possibilities.

For example, you've been sitting at home, waiting for someone to call. You wait and you wait, and the phone doesn't ring. Your automatic reaction is to assume that the other person obviously doesn't like you. The situation is viewed in the worst possible light. Challenge yourself to consider if there might be another reason for the silence. Could he or she be extremely busy? Perhaps there has been a personal emergency. Did he or she lose your number? The optimist would initiate a call him or herself. He or she might get rejected, but there are always other opportunities. When faced with the choice to act or not, ask yourself, "What have I got to lose?"

2. Take a look at the people with whom you surround yourself. It's true that misery does love company. Like a bad cold, negative thinking is contagious. Pessimistic friends and family may be dragging you down in ways you don't immediately recognize. Make it a habit to notice people's attitude. Then surround yourself with as many optimists as you can. The truth is, optimism is as contagious as pessimism.

3. Sad to say, the news these days could turn Pollyanna into the Grinch. It seems that every report predicts disaster. Bad news sells, so the networks are happy to deliver. But how much of this news actually affects you directly? Probably very little. Remain informed but limit your exposure to the news. If a particular issue is of interest, find something with whom to discuss it instead of remaining glued to one of the 24/7 broadcasters who will happily keep you in a state of fear.

4. Keep a journal for positive thoughts and write in it every night. It needn't be anything spectacular, like winning the lottery or getting a promotion. A journal will remind you of the little joys you experience every day – the aroma of that first cup of coffee in the morning; getting a seat on a crowded bus; the

nice person who held the door for you. It's easy to overlook these little pleasures when we are focused on negatives.

Becoming increasingly aware of the positive aspects of our lives helps us become happier on a very basic level.

While you are at it, take notice of your own random acts of kindness. Did you help a neighbor with his or her packages? Did you hold the elevator for someone? Get in touch with your own positive acts.

5. Some things we can control, others we cannot. That is life. You can't control your company going out of business and you being unemployed. What you are able to control is your reaction. Will you panic and blame bad luck? Will you start to network and look for new opportunities? Will you go on an eating and drinking binge? How you handle adversity can easily determine your future.

Losing a job is hard, but it's not the end. It just might be the beginning of something exciting.

6. Being an optimist doesn't mean not acknowledging problems. If you lose your job and respond with, "Oh, well, something will turn up," you aren't being realistic. Yes, opportunities *do* lie ahead, but it is up to you to make them happen. Consider your strengths and weaknesses and how you can best be an asset to a company. Acknowledge that money

45

may be tight for a while and draw up a balanced budget. An optimist believes good things will happen but is prepared for the bumps along the way.

CHAPTER 6

OPTIMISM AND GRATITUDE

In the previous chapter, we discussed how an optimistic attitude is everything. Let's take this a step further. There are two crucial ingredients to a positive attitude – gratitude and self-confidence. The more you enhance these personal qualities, the greater your optimism is likely to be. Gratitude and self-confidence are the building blocks that make optimism possible.

This chapter and the following one will show the benefits of gratitude and self-confidence and how we can use these traits to enjoy the benefits of a more optimistic life.

1. Gratitude makes us more approachable and likeable. An attitude of gratefulness is appreciated by those around us and draws people to us. It makes us nicer and more pleasant. People

who spend their lives complaining are usually viewed to be annoying and unfriendly.

2. Gratitude increases our on-the-job effectiveness. Managers who don't show appreciation for their employees are seen as less effective and rate less loyalty. Managers who encourage their staff with praise, recognition, and financial rewards hold on to their valuable workers and help increase overall production. Sixty-five percent of workers feel their efforts are not noticed or appreciated.

3. Gratitude keeps our emotions in balance and prevents negative thoughts from becoming overwhelming. One of the primary obstacles to gratitude is envy, that underlying fear that someone may have something that we don't.

Envy happens when we compare ourselves to someone else. When we begin such a comparison, we are far more likely to become less satisfied and optimistic with our own existence. Practicing gratitude is the best antidote to envy.

4. Gratitude makes us less self-centered. Pessimists tend to be self- centered. Everything revolves about their fears and how to protect themselves against the next disaster, which they are

sure is lurking around the corner. Other people and their feelings are rarely given much thought. Gratitude shifts our mental focus from ourselves to others. That is why optimists are easier to approach, as a rule.

5. Gratitude increases our self-esteem, which in turns makes us more optimistic. It's the parts working as a whole.

We are surrounded by messages that we aren't enough every day. We need the right clothes, the appropriate job title, the latest car, and access to the most fashionable restaurants. We should look a certain way and be thin and gorgeous, with thousands of likes on Instagram. Advertisers certainly go far in bringing forth this message. If we don't live up to these artificial standards, we aren't quite "good enough." Many of us aren't even aware of how we may be influenced by these messages.

This can be hard on a person's self-esteem. Pessimists may frantically try to keep up, trying one self-improvement method after another, only to become depressed when faced with failure. They strive for perfection, and that is the opposite of optimism. By developing self-esteem, optimists feel good about themselves, regardless of where they are in life. They are "enough" at any point in time. Of course, they can work for more, and usually do. But their self-esteem is never dependent on material goods. It's a feeling that optimists cultivate deep within themselves. They are grateful for what they have right now, and grateful for the possibility of having more in the future.

6. Gratitude helps us enjoy a better night's sleep. Optimists spend less time worrying and more time actively pursuing their goals, so their mind is at ease. They fall asleep quicker and enjoy a more peaceful night's rest.

7. Gratitude helps us cope with adversities. Optimists are more likely to be pro-active in their actions when things go wrong than pessimists.

8. Gratitude changes how we remember the past. We may think of memories as absolutes, but they are rarely set in stone. Pessimists can remember the past as being bleak, as in, "I was always miserable," "I was never hugged." The problem with "always" and "never" is that they can distort memories and block out the good as we focus only on the bad. Many times, we remember past incidences worse than they were. When we practice gratitude, we activate a mental switch that not only makes the present more positive but creates a more positive past. In that respect, we can indeed change the past. This lessen the

grip that the past has over us and allows us to let go and enjoy the present and plan for a better future.

According to Cicero, the ancient Roman philosopher, "Gratitude is not only the greatest of virtues, but the parent of all the others." When we have gratitude, we can make anything else possible. Studies have shown that grateful people interpret events differently than less grateful people. A study of students who were given aid and assistance of some sort found that grateful students perceive their benefactors far more favorable than non-grateful students. Pessimists invariably find reason to complain, and that makes gratitude very difficult. When we feel grateful, we also feel closer to others. For pessimists, who are always looking for the worst, this can be a scary proposition. Being close to people makes them vulnerable.

Letting More Gratitude into Your Life

In the not too distant past, gratitude was expected. Thank you letters and reciprocal kindness were the norm. Regrettably, this is becoming a lost art. Grandparents and givers of gifts wait in vain for a note, or even a phone call, of appreciation and gratitude. Brides complain that the value of their wedding gift wasn't enough to cover the cost of the meal. What once was good manners is slowly becoming the exception.

This situation does not speak well for future generations. A recent Twitter rant highlighted the extent to which many people today lack gratitude and optimism. A young woman had received a number of Christmas presents from an aunt. Instead of simply saying "thank you," said young lady ranted about how the aunt should have given her gift cards instead of "forcing" her to accept the aunt's choices, and that the aunt was stupid and thoughtless and certainly wouldn't be receiving any thank you for her "horrendous and thoughtless" actions. To say that this is an unhappy and miserable young woman would be an understatement. Talk about focusing on the negative …

Fortunately, gratitude is still in vogue in many circles, and there are actions you can take to boost your gratitude quotient.

It's Easy to be More Grateful

It doesn't take a lot of time or money to feel gratitude, and the benefits of increasing our positive thinking are immeasurable.

1. Start by saying thank you more. Show gratitude to your loved ones for being in your life. Say thank you to the waiter or clerk who has contributed to your day in many intangible ways.

Genuinely feel the gratitude. We spend one day a year, Thanksgiving, giving thanks. Make every day your own Thanksgiving Day.

2. Focus on the moment. Truly appreciate the food you are eating instead of worrying about a report while not tasting what you are eating. Enjoy the sunshine instead of worrying when it will begin to rain. Simply be quiet for a few minutes and embrace all of the abundance and goodness around you.

3. No one does snail mail anymore. So, imagine the surprise when you write to an old teacher, neighbor, co-worker who has made a difference in your life. It doesn't have to be

anything elaborate. A simple, "Thanks for being you," will make someone's day.

4. Make gratitude a habit. Set aside a few minutes every day to remember all the reasons you have to be thankful. Reviewing your day before going to bed is the best time to do this.

5. Switch ingratitude to gratitude. When you find yourself fuming because the bus is late, imagine that there aren't any buses and you'd have to walk. Does the long line at the market make you feel impatient? Imagine there were no supermarkets and you have to walk from small store to small store for hours. Does your best friend drive you crazy occasionally? Imagine the thousands of lonely people without companionship. It's easy to feel gratitude when you simply turn that mental switch.

6. Avoid being judgmental. We unconsciously judge people daily without knowing all the facts about them. Did you co-worker snap at you? Maybe she has a sick child at home or in the hospital. Did you neighbor fail to acknowledge your greeting? Perhaps he or she is worried about losing his or her job. It's smart to assume someone else's behavior has nothing to do with you until you find out otherwise.

CHAPTER 7

OPTIMISM AND SELF- CONFIDENCE

Along with gratitude, self-confidence is the other foundation necessary for optimism. According to psychologist Nathaniel Branden, "Of all the judgments we pass in life, none is more important than the judgment we pass on ourselves."

Self-confidence is an evaluation of our basic worth. It's a predisposition to seeing ourselves as able to cope with life's many challenges. It is the belief that we *can* and *should* be happy. With self-confidence, we move toward our goals; without it, we retreat into denial, excuses, and fear. When we lack self-confidence, our thoughts and actions are rarely rooted in reality.

When we are self-confident, we act in ways that benefit us, which in turn increases our self-confidence and optimism.

To boost our self-confidence, it is necessary to question negative beliefs. If your belief in yourself was damaged while growing up, this isn't always easy. These beliefs have become ingrained in our mind. The cause can be incompetent parenting, friends that were bullies, or other traumas. The important thing to understand is that no one has to remain a victim. We have a choice about how we think about ourselves. As an adult, you can rid your brain of the negativity that has been holding you back. You have the ability to feel better about yourself and your future. It's all about the choices you make.

1. People who lack self-confidence are terrified of rejection, because they are apt to take it personally. As a result, it's easier to avoid rejection by not trying. The more you

don't try, the weaker your sense of self-confidence. It's important to "put yourself out there." Rejection is a normal part of life. Ask yourself what the worse scenario would be if you experienced rejection. Would your life end if your attractive neighbor won't go out with you? What would happen if you went on an interview and didn't get the job?

The fact is, very little would change in our lives following a rejection unless we allow it to. Once you realize how powerless rejection actually is, it becomes easier to keep trying. The more you try, the more you grow your optimism.

2. Every morning, determine to do just one single thing that we shift you out of your comfort zone. Ask a co-worker to lunch. Chat with an attractive stranger while standing in line. You don't need to change the world, just your own attitude. Every time you complete a small goal, it assures your brain that you can accomplish things. Once you accept that as truth, the goals will become larger and more important.

3. Many people who advocate optimism and self-confidence suggest that you focus on dealing with improving your weaknesses. However, everyone has a weakness or two. Begin to focus on increasing your strengths, instead. If you are

good with numbers, offer to take on more of the financial matters at the office. You love to cook? Become the gourmet chef to your family and friends. Honing your strengths will make you view yourself as more competent.

4. Dwelling on past failures and mistakes can be a real self- confidence robber. Everyone experiences failure or makes mistakes, but when you keep reliving it in your own mind, you simply keep failure alive by having a constant negative dialogue with yourself. Instead, consciously distract yourself through other activities. Join a gym. Learn a new skill. Find a volunteer activity you enjoy. By expanding your focus, your mind will stop obsessing about the past.

5. Stop comparing yourself to your peers. Here's the reality: there will *always* be someone with a better job, more friends, more money, and better looks. That is simply a fact. Concentrate on who you are, instead. Granted, it can be frustrating when a colleague gets the promotion you wanted or when a friend is offered a dream job. Ultimately, however, what does that have to do with you? Absolutely nothing. Focus on your own unique self and your own goals. Use self-confidence to

create your own path to success. Never let someone else determine your self-worth.

6. Appearance isn't everything, but don't overlook the effect of good grooming in the way you see yourself. A neat, clean appearance, a sharp outfit can be an immediate confidence booster.

7. Exercise can be a great confidence enhancer as it provides you with measurable results. If you begin to jog, you might have difficulty running for half a mile. As you continue, you will yourself doing a full mile, then further. Karate and other self- defense classes can serve the same purpose. Success is measurable as you earn higher-level belts. Nothing enhances your self-confidence than seeing actual results.

It is definitely possible to grow your self-confidence through daily positive habits. As your self-confidence increases, so does your optimism.

CHAPTER 8

DAILY OPTIMISM HABITS

Optimism will enhance your life. It is the necessary ingredient for happiness and success. As we've discussed, the good news is that we are able to shift our mindset from negative to positive by making better choices and becoming more aware of our thoughts and actions.

In addition to making changes in the way we think, there are countless small daily habits that will keep our optimism thriving. These are life-affirming steps that help us find the buried treasures in every single day.

1. Smile more. It's as simple as that. You'll be surprised at the difference it makes in your day.

2. Find something funny. Instead of watching the dreaded news, tune in to a good comedy. People who laugh live longer.

3. Make a list of all the people on whom you can depend. As you become more optimistic, watch that list grow.

4. Leave a hidden note for your spouse or your kids. Know that you've made their day.

5. Do a good deed. Help someone with their bundles. Let someone ahead in line at the grocers. Karma will hit you back when you're not looking

6. Pamper yourself. Occasionally, treat yourself to something special, whether a night out in a ritzy restaurant or a splurge outfit.

7. Develop a tradition, whether it's Sunday dinner, weekend brunch, or Wednesday family game night.

8. Listen to your favorite song once a day.

9. Explore a street or neighborhood that is unfamiliar to you. Maybe it has something nice to offer.

10. Pessimist sometimes find it difficult to bond with people. Become more sociable. Spend five minutes chatting with someone in the lunchroom. Ask the checkout clerk how his or her day is going. Say hi to the bus driver. Optimistic people are genuinely interested in others.

11. View duties as privileges. We all have things we "have" to do, whether its go to work, pay the bills, or clean our house. Most of us wish we could avoid these chores. We can when we change "have to" to "are able to." You are "able" to go to work because you have a job. You are "able" to pay the bills because you earn a salary. You are "able" to clean the house because you are fortunate to have a nice place to live. Shifting from one word to another makes a huge difference in how we perceive our lives.

12. Do the crossword puzzle. It's fun, and it provides you with an instant sense of accomplishment.

13. You make choices every day. Start to question each choice (such as where to have lunch, etc.) and ask yourself how and if it benefits you. Consider *all* your options. One pessimist had breakfast at the same diner for years because change of any kind unnerved him.

14. Make a list about everything you don't like in your life. You may not be able to fix all, but you should be able to turn some of them around.

15. Candles can hold a special power. Light one or two for dinner or during a relaxing bath.

16. Music and dance can touch the soul. Listen to some uplifting melody every change you have. And move those feet. Even if you're a klutz, it's impossible not to feel happy when dancing. Take a class, learn to line dance or square dance.

17. Start each day with a purpose. It can be as simple as finishing a report or going to the park for lunch. But follow through on your plan. It's another way to see accomplishments come to fruition.

18. Read books about successful people who dared to dream. It will inspire you to do the same.

19. Stress can make optimism difficult. How can you feel optimistic when your mind is bogged down with a litany of worries? Develop the habit of daily meditation, which is proven to be a tremendous stress reliever. Simply find a quiet place, close your eyes, and focus on your breathing for 15 minutes to half an hour. By clearing your brain of negativism, you are able to focus on more positive aspectsof your life.

20. Tell yourself every day, "When I change my thinking, I change my life."

CONCLUSION

Living a more optimist life will increase your health, make you happier, improve your relationships, and help you achieve your dreams. It's all about how you view and approach life. When surrounded by lemons, the optimist learns to make lemonade.

- Enjoy improved health and a longer life by ridding yourself of negativity.

- Lead others by example. People enjoy being around optimists and are inspired by their success. That is the reason optimists have more friends and make more effective leaders. They lead through inspiration.

- When you are optimistic, you persevere. You may need to work hard to reach your goal, but you always keep it in sight.

- Pessimists spend their life worrying about what could go wrong. Optimists spend their time thinking about how to do things better.

- Life can be unpredictable, and everyone feels down at times. During tough times, remind yourself of all you have instead of complaining about what you lack. Attitude is everything.

- When remaining truly optimistic becomes difficult, fake it. Reality will catch up soon enough.

- When planning your goals, remind yourself of what you have already accomplished. This will keep your mind positive to future possibilities.

• Reward yourself for optimistic thoughts and actions. It will serve as a reminder to continue thinking positively.

• Being optimistic is easier when you feel your best. Make exercise and eating healthy a daily habit. Lack of exercise and unhealthy eating habits will drag you down.

• The past is gone, and we don't know the future. Refuse to dwell on past mistakes or injustices, as bitterness can overwhelm you with negativity. Just let it go. And don't waste time fretting about the unknown future but prepare yourself for unlimited abundance.

• You don't live on a deserted island. Enhance your gratitude by helping others.

• Relationships take work. Only pessimists expect perfect relationships. Optimists take the necessary steps to *create* happy and loving relationships.

• Optimism is about the choices you make every day. Choose wisely.

• Stop focusing on the news, which is filled with negativism. Read a book, instead.

• Don't focus on problems; look for solutions.

• Gratitude and self-confidence are the foundation of optimism. The more you enhance these traits, the more optimistic you will feel.

• Practice optimism every day. Small steps lead to a great journey.

Printed by Libri Plureos GmbH in Hamburg, Germany